ALFRED's
SACRED PERFORMER
COLLECTIONS

Open My Heart to Worship

MW01041458

Arranged by Mark Hayes

11 of the Most Popular Praise and Worship Songs Masterfully Arranged for Solo Piano

My first experience with praise and worship music was in 1977. I was the music editor for Tempo Music Publications and we published a chorus book entitled *Scripture in Song*, compiled by David and Dale Garrett of Auckland, New Zealand. The Garretts were some of the early pioneers in writing scripture-based choruses that were accessible to congregations. In the 1990s, another publisher asked me to write a series of piano solo collections called *Lord, Be Glorified*, which seemed to really speak to pianists and churches alike, all across the country. Now, almost thirty years and many piano books later, I am pleased to continue this tradition with the Alfred Publishing Company.

Open My Heart to Worship contains some of the top praise and worship songs of the last six or seven years, songs that are now part of the "canon" of contemporary and blended worshipers. I've reached back even farther with a few selections such as "They'll Know We Are Christians by Our Love," "Sweet, Sweet Spirit" and "Surely the Presence of the Lord Is in This Place."

I have purposely arranged these songs in the keys in which they are usually sung. With a little editing, some of these arrangements could even be used to accompany your congregation. I've included chord symbols throughout for those people who want to improvise beyond the written notes on the page.

Whether old or new, I hope the songs I've arranged will create a space for the Holy Spirit to minister to you and your listeners, so all may open their hearts to worship.

Mark Hayes

Alfred

ABOVE ALL

Words and Music by
Paul Baloche and Lenny LeBlanc
Arranged by Mark Hayes

Slowly, with a steady rhythm ($\quarternote$ = ca. 69)

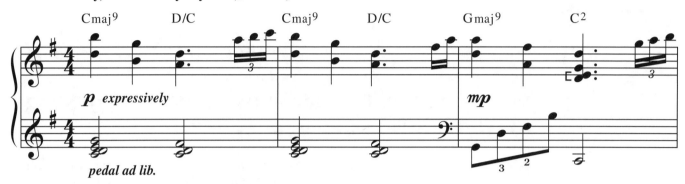

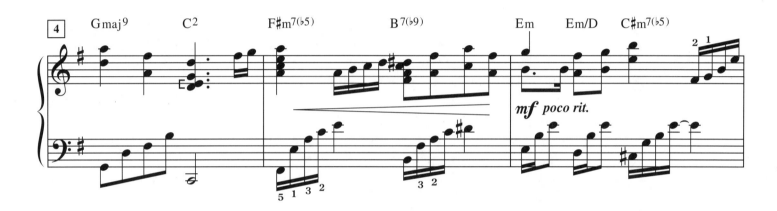

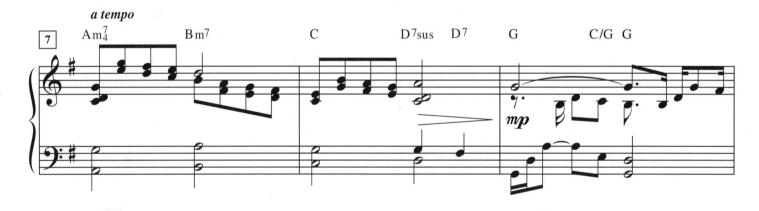

6

Draw Me Close

Words and Music by Kelly Carpenter
Arranged by Mark Hayes

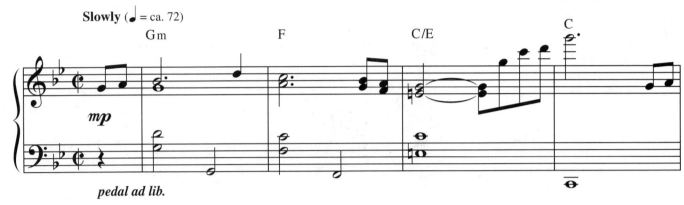

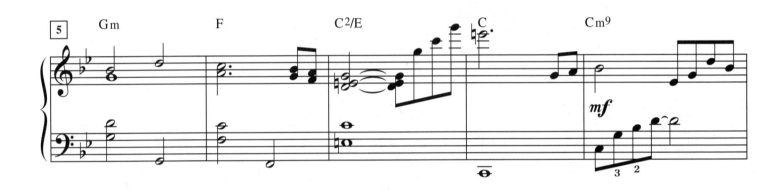

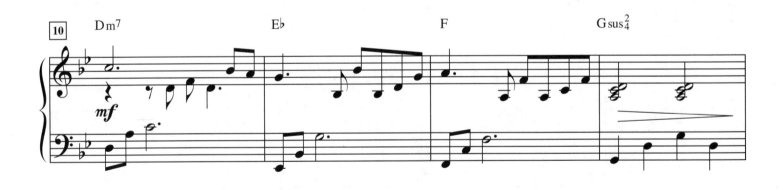

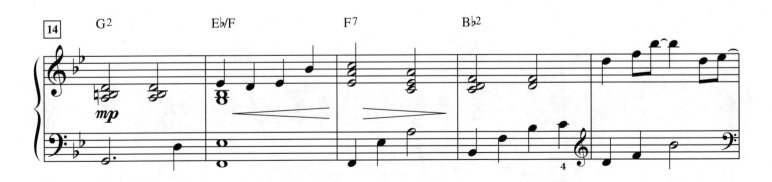

10

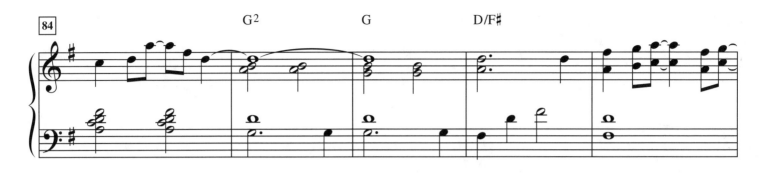

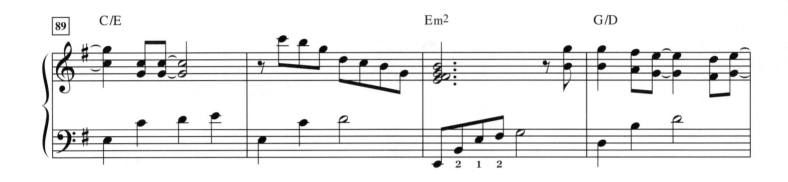

THE HEART OF WORSHIP

Words and Music by Matt Redman
Arranged by Mark Hayes

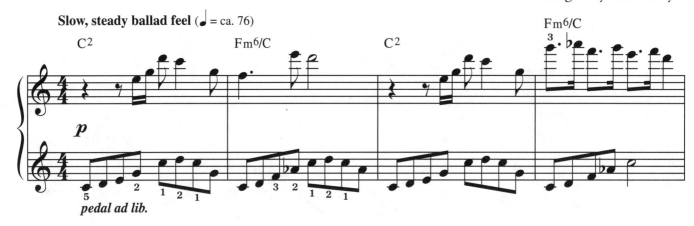

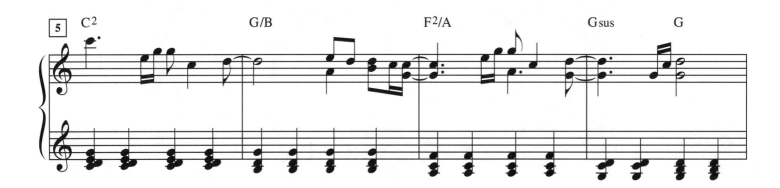

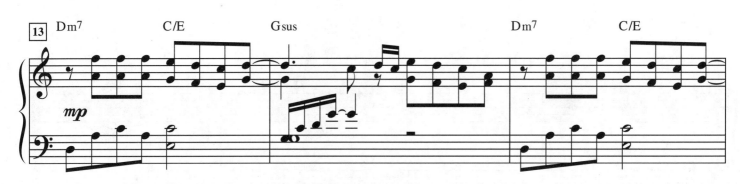

BREATHE

Words and Music by Marie Barnett
Arranged by Mark Hayes

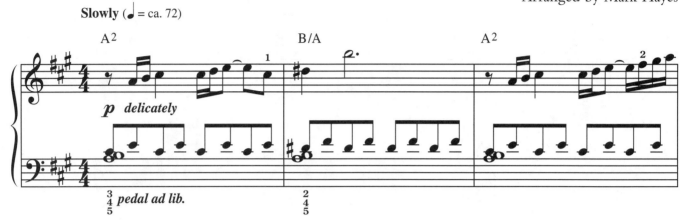

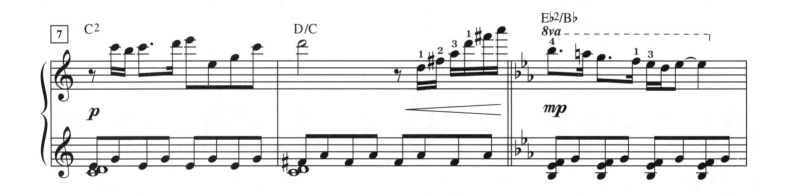

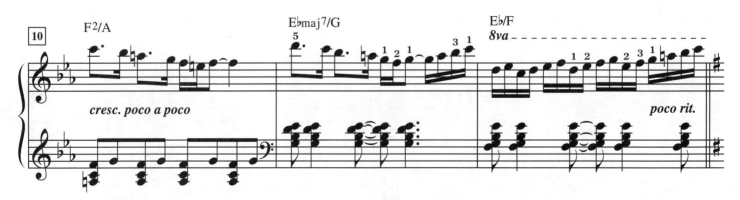

Here I Am to Worship

Words and Music by Tim Hughes
Arranged by Mark Hayes

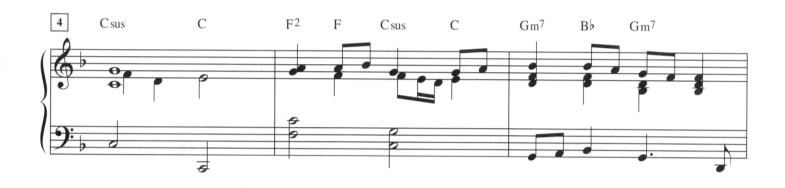

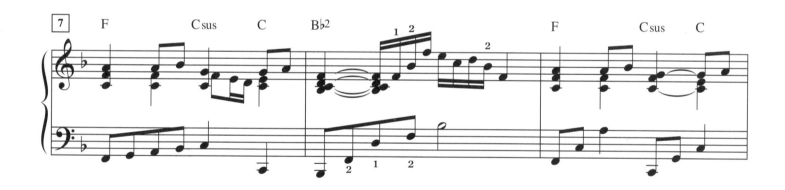

25

26

In the Presence of Jehovah
with
Surely the Presence of the Lord Is in This Place

Arranged by Mark Hayes

"In the Presence of Jehovah"
Words and Music by Geron and Becky Davis

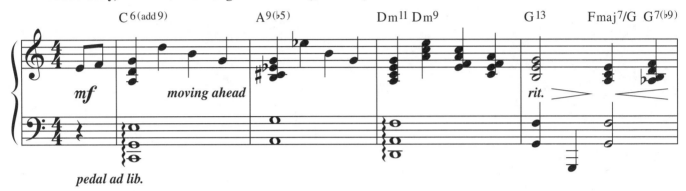

"Surely the Presence of the Lord Is in This Place"
Words and Music by Lanny Wolfe

Knowing You

(All I Once Held Dear)

Words and Music by Graham Kendrick
Arranged by Mark Hayes

34

35

Let Everything That Has Breath

Words and Music by Matt Redman
Arranged by Mark Hayes

41

OPEN THE EYES OF MY HEART
WITH
BE THOU MY VISION

Arranged by Mark Hayes

"Open the Eyes of My Heart"
Words and Music by Paul Baloche

Moderately (♩ = 116)

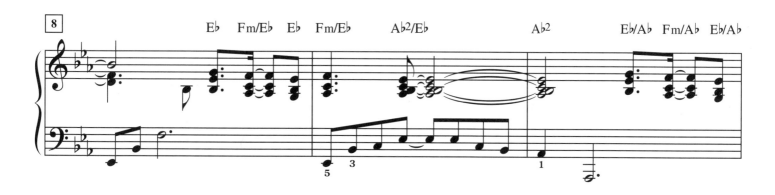

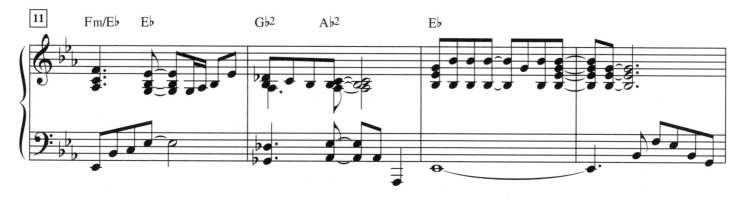

44

"Be Thou My Vision"
Traditional Irish

Sweet, Sweet Spirit

Words and Music by Doris Akers
Arranged by Mark Hayes

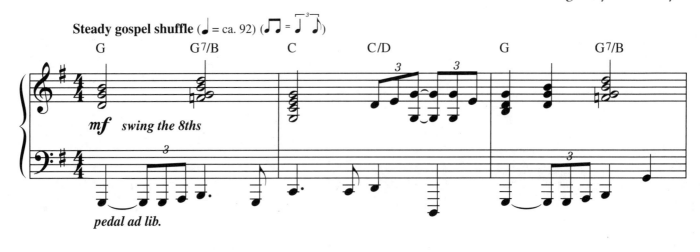

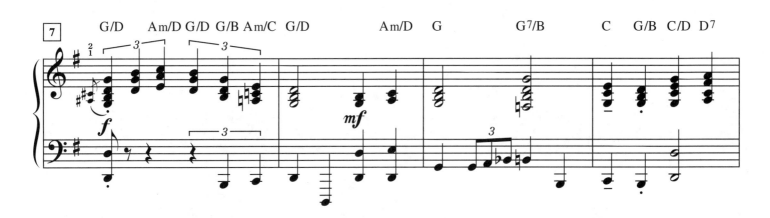

49

They'll Know We Are Christians by Our Love

Words and Music by Peter Scholtes
Arranged by Mark Hayes

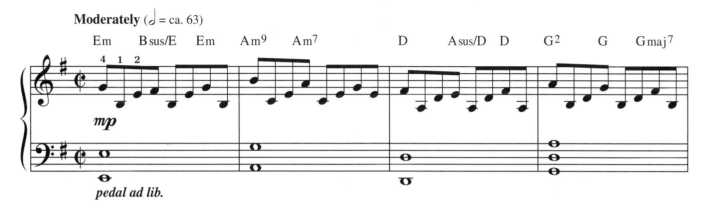

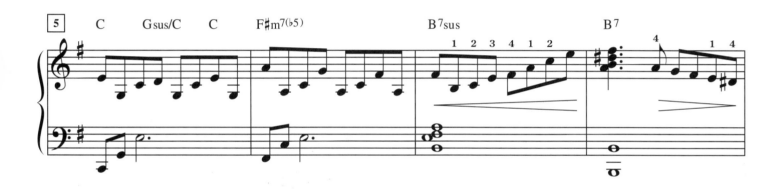

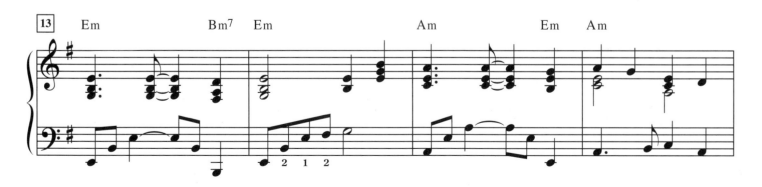

56

ABOVE ALL

Above all powers, above all kings,
Above all nature and all created things;
Above all wisdom and all the ways of man,
You were here before the world began.
Above all kingdoms, above all thrones,
Above all wonders the world has ever known;
Above all wealth and treasures of the earth,
There's no way to measure what You're worth.

Crucified, laid behind the stone;
You lived to die, rejected and alone;
Like a rose trampled on the ground,
You took the fall and thought of me above all.

DRAW ME CLOSE

Draw me close to You,
Never let me go.
I lay it all down again
To hear You say that I'm Your friend.

You are my desire,
No one else will do.
'Cause nothing else could take Your place;
To feel the warmth of Your embrace.
Help me find the way,
Bring me back to You.

You're all I want,
You're all I ever needed.
You're all I want-
Help me know You are near.

BREATHE

This is the air I breathe,
This is the air I breathe,
Your holy presence, living in me.
This is my daily bread,
This is my daily bread,
Your very Word spoken to me.

And I, I'm desperate for You,
And I, I'm lost without You.

This is the air I breathe.

THE HEART OF WORSHIP

When the music fades,
All is stripped away,
And I simply come:
Longing just to bring
Something that's of worth
That will bless Your heart.

I'll bring You more than a song,
For a song in itself is not what You have required.
You search much deeper within
Through the way things appear.
You're looking into my heart.

Chorus:
I'm coming back to the heart of worship,
And it's all about You,
It's all about You, Jesus.
I'm sorry, Lord, for the thing I've made it,
When it's all about You,
It's all about You, Jesus.

King of endless worth,
No one could express
How much You deserve.
Though I'm weak and poor,
All I have is Yours,
Every single breath.
I'll bring You more than a song,
For a song in itself is not what You have required.
You search much deeper within
Through the way things appear.
You're looking into my heart.

Chorus

HERE I AM TO WORSHIP

Light of the world, You stepped down into darkness,
Opened my eyes, let me see.
Beauty that made this heart adore You,
Hope of a life spent with You.

Chorus:
Here I am to worship,
Here I am to bow down,
Here I am to say that You're my God.
You're altogether lovely,
Altogether worthy,
Altogether wonderful to me.
King of all days, oh so highly exalted,
Glorious in heaven above.
Humbly You came to the earth You created,
All for love's sake became poor.

Chorus

And I'll never know how much it cost to see
My sin upon that cross.

Chorus

IN THE PRESENCE OF JEHOVAH

In the presence of Jehovah,
God Almighty, Prince of Peace;
Troubles vanish, hearts are mended
In the presence of the King.

SURELY THE PRESENCE OF THE LORD IS IN THIS PLACE

Surely the presence of the Lord is in this place.
I can feel His mighty power and His grace.
I can hear the brush of angels' wings,
I see glory on each face;
Surely the presence of the Lord is in this place.

KNOWING YOU (All I Once Held Dear)

All I once held dear, built my life upon,
All this world reveres and wars to own,
All I once thought gain I have counted loss,
Spent and worthless now compared to this:
Chorus:
Knowing You, Jesus, knowing You-
There is no greater thing.
You're my all, You're the best,
You're my joy, my righteousness
And I love You, Lord.

Now my heart's desire is to know You more,
To be found in You and known as Yours.
To possess by faith what I could not earn,
All surpassing gift of righteousness.

Chorus

Oh, to know the power of Your risen life
And to know You in Your sufferings,
To become like You in Your death, my Lord,
So with You to live and never die.

Chorus

LET EVERYTHING THAT HAS BREATH

Chorus:
Let everything that, everything that,
Everything that has breath praise the Lord.
Let everything that, everything that,
Everything that has breath praise the Lord.
Praise You in the mornin',
Praise You in the evenin',
Praise You when I'm young and when I'm old.
Praise You when I'm laughin',
Praise You when I'm grievin',
Praise You every season of the soul.
If we could see how much You're worth,
Your power, Your might, Your endless love,
Then surely we would never cease to praise.

Chorus

Praise You in the heavens,
Joining with the angels,
Praising You forever and a day.
Praise You on the earth now,
Joining with creation,
Calling all the nations to Your praise.
If we could see how much You're worth,
Your power, Your might, Your endless love,
Then surely we would never cease to praise.

Chorus

OPEN THE EYES OF MY HEART

Open the eyes of my heart, Lord,
Open the eyes of my heart;
I want to see You,
I want to see You,

Open the eyes of my heart, Lord,
Open the eyes of my heart;
I want to see You,
I want to see You,

To see You high and lifted up,
Shining in the light of Your glory.
Pour out Your power and love
As we sing, Holy, holy, holy.

Holy, holy, holy,
Holy, holy, holy,
Holy, holy, holy,
I want to see You.

Holy, holy, holy,
Holy, holy, holy,
Holy, holy, holy,
I want to see You.

BE THOU MY VISION

Traditional Irish
Translation by Mary E. Byrne
Versified by Eleanor H. Hull
Harmonization by David Evans
Arranged by Mark Hayes

Be Thou my vision, O Lord of my heart;
Naught be all else to me save that Thou art;
Thou my best thought, by day or by night,
Waking or sleeping, Thy presence my light.

Be Thou my wisdom, and Thou my true word;
I ever with Thee and Thou with me, Lord;
Thou my great Father, I Thy true son,
Thou in me dwelling, and I with Thee one.

SWEET, SWEET SPIRIT

Words and Music by Doris Akers

There's a sweet, sweet Spirit in this place,
And I know that it's the Spirit of the Lord.
There are sweet expressions on each face,
And I know they feel the presence of the Lord.
Chorus:
Sweet Holy Spirit, sweet heavenly Dove,
Stay right here with us, filling us with Your love.
And for these blessings we lift our hearts in praise.
Without a doubt we'll know that we have been revived
When we shall leave this place.

There are blessings you cannot receive
Till you know Him in His fullness, and believe.
You're the one to profit when you say,
"I am going to walk with Jesus all the way."

Chorus

THEY'LL KNOW WE ARE CHRISTIANS BY OUR LOVE

Words and Music by Peter Scholtes

We are one in the Spirit; we are one in the Lord.
We are one in the Spirit; we are one in the Lord.
And we pray that all unity may one day be restored.
And they'll know we are Christians by our love, by our love.
Yes, they'll know we are Christians by our love.

We will walk with each other; we will walk hand in hand.
We will walk with each other; we will walk hand in hand.
And together we'll spread the news that God is in our land.
And they'll know we are Christians by our love, by our love.
Yes, they'll know we are Christians by our love.

We will work with each other; we will work side by side.
We will work with each other; we will work side by side.
And we'll guard each one's dignity and save each one's pride.
And they'll know we are Christians by our love, by our love.
Yes, they'll know we are Christians by our love.

All praise to the Father, from whom all things come.
And all praise to Christ Jesus, His only Son.
And all praise to the Spirit, who makes us one.
And they'll know we are Christians by our love, by our love.
Yes, they'll know we are Christians by our love.